There's no greater testimonial to South Dakota's profound beauty and geological diversity than the land itself. But perhaps one of the state's earliest explorers said it best: "Let it not be supposed, that life on these boundless regions is monotonous and dreary, for nowhere does nature sit more majestically enthroned...."

Hewn from the granite of South Dakota's Black Hills, the heads of four great American presidents are carved on Mount Rushmore. As a tribute to the ideals of the nation, the world's largest sculpture commemorates the selfless contributions of George Washington, Thomas Jefferson, Abraham Lincoln, and Theodore Roosevelt.

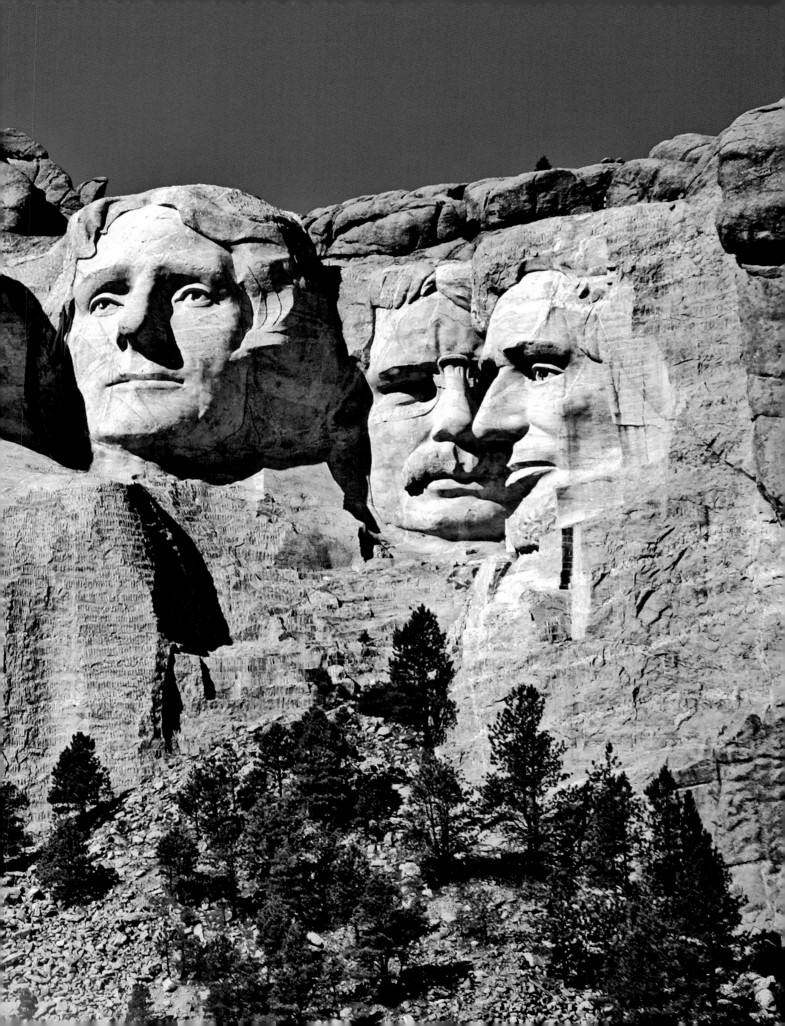

American sculptor Gutzon Borglum was born on March 25, 1867 in St. Charles, Idaho Territory. Though art was his lifelong passion, Borglum – the man – was one of many dimensions. He was a poet, an engineer and an inventor. By all accounts he was the truest definition of statesman and patriot.

His original plans, which included the presidents to their waists, along with a history museum, were never completed. Before his Rushmore dream could be fully realized, Borglum died on March 6, 1941. He was 73. His son finished carving that October, bringing work of the Shrine of Democracy to an end. At nearly the same hour, one of the nation's greatest fights for our Republic began with the country entering World War II.

With every blast of dynamite, every bore of the drill, and each drive of a chisel, the vision of state historian Doane Robinson and sculptor Gutzon Borglum came another step closer to reality. Carving began in the summer of 1927 and continued to the spring of 1941 when Borglum died. His son Lincoln Borglum directed the completion of the monument to its present state later that year. The use of a ½th scale model enabled Borglum to carve the granite figures in accurate proportion. A protractor – like device called a "pointer" measured one foot of rock for every inch of the artist's model.

Gutzon Borglum's Model of Mt. Rushmore Memorial – Washington, Jefferson, Roosevelt & Lincoln – RISE STUDIO 675

MOUNT RUSHMORE

Some 800 million pounds of rock were removed with dynamite, jackhammers and pneumatic drills during the memorials creation. With this colossal undertaking came problems of even greater magnitude including poor quality granite and surface rock erosion. Thus, plans constantly changed. Originally Jefferson was to be placed on Washington's right with the other presidents to his left. Due to flaws in the stone, Jefferson's figure was destroyed at half-completion and restarted on Washington's left. On Independence Day 1930 the figure of first president George Washington was dedicated as a symbol of our nation's founding. The 60-foot figure faces east, capturing the day's first light. It was at the Jefferson dedication on August 30, 1936, that Franklin D. Roosevelt was touched in the deepest sense by the magnificence of Mount Rushmore. "I had seen the photographs and the drawings of this great work," he said, "and yet, until about ten minutes ago, I had no conception of its magnitude, its permanent beauty and its importance." A fitting time for the dedication of Abraham Lincoln was September 17, 1937, the 150th anniversary of the adoption of the US constitution. Theodore Roosevelt was dedicated on July 12, 1939.

Minor surface blemishes call for careful and consistent maintenance of the memorial. A water-resistant silicone formula is used by the National Park Service to repair any cracks that develop. It was Borglum's wish that the granite figures remain "until the wind and rain alone shall wash them away."

Amid staunch protests from engineers, Senator Peter Norbeck pushed and succeeded in building his Iron Mountain Road. With the construction of pigtail bridges and tunnels, the scenic byway – once called the "impossible road" – allowed for even greater views of Mount Rushmore and the surrounding Black Hills.

Iron Creek
Tunnel

SYLVAN LAKE

CUSTER STATE PARK

Custer State park is home to a herd of bison, numbering in excess of 1,000 head. The size of the herd is kept stable by the annual bison roundup and auction, where every year several hundred are sold at auction so that the park will not become overpopulated with these magnificent animals.

The bison share the parks 71,000 acres with other wildlife as well, including elk, deer, mountain goats, pronghorn, bighorn sheep and prairie dogs. In addition to wildlife watching, there is first-rate trout fishing, swimming and boating at the four mountain lakes of the park; Sylvan Lake, Stockdale Lake, Legion Lake and Center Lake.

Custer State Park is also home to a band of begging burros who appear to enjoy their self-appointed role as park ambassadors. Seemingly appreciative of a gentle pat on the head, they are frequently seen nuzzling beside car windows of those visiting the park.

The glow of a late afternoon sun is cast on the Cathedral Spires, creating perhaps one of South Dakota's most breathtaking images. For eons – 500 million years or more – the Black Hills have been in the making, with the last 100 million years bringing forth the creation of the Cathedral Spires. The stone shafts, thought to resemble pipe organs, were later coined "Needles." Today these spires are the major topographic feature of the region.

One of the more interesting features on the Needles Highway is Needles Eye.

In the midst of the 71,000-acre Custer State Park is the glittering gem, Sylvan Lake, one of the most scenic lakes of the Black Hills. The lake and vicinity are favored for resorts, camping, fishing, hiking and boating opportunities. Trail rides are popular given the wealth of wildlife inhabiting the park, the most visible being the large herd of free roaming bison.

One thousand five hundred feet above Mount Rushmore lies Black Elk Peak. Formerly called Harney Peak, the name was changed on August 11, 2016.

A stone building erected atop Black Elk Peak in 1935-1938 was the work of the Civilian Conservation Corps, where for three decades it served as a manned fire tower.

Black Elk Peak is revered for its spectacular granite pinnacles and incredible vistas. At 7,242 feet above sea level, the summit is the highest point in the United States east of the Rocky Mountains. From the peak, the views are truly spectacular encompassing 5,000 square miles of mountains and plains that sprawl over western South Dakota, Nebraska and Wyoming.

Sculptor Korczak Ziolkowski (1908-1982) was born in Boston of Polish descent. He endured a difficult upbringing and became a self-taught and renowned sculptor. Chief Henry Standing Bear invited Korczak to the Black Hills to carve Crazy Horse. After much consideration, Korczak accepted. Ruth Ross (1926-2014) followed Korczak, they were married and had ten children who took part in the Dream of Crazy Horse as they were growing up.

Today, dedicated staff, including some Ziolkowski children and grandchildren, carry on the project which includes the Mountain Carving in progress, The Indian Museum of North America®, and The Indian University of North America®. The mission of Crazy Horse Memorial Foundation is to protect and preserve the culture, tradition, and living heritage of all North American Indians.

WIND CAVE NATIONAL PARK

Wind Cave is the 6th longest cave in the world and is the centerpiece of Wind Cave National Park. A network of underground caverns stretch for over 123 miles with many parts yet to be explored. Unlike the more common stalactites and stalagmites found in most caves, Wind Cave is filled with strange and wonderful formations created by the crystallization of calcite. Delicate features, known as "boxwork" that resemble honeycombs, popcorn and frostwork decorate the ever-changing cave interior.

Differences in atmospheric pressure above and below ground cause a whistling wind at the cave's only natural opening. This whistling coming from a 10-inch opening is what led to the cave's discovery by Jesse and Tom Bingham in 1881. It was established as a National Park in South Dakota on January 9, 1903.

JEWEL CAVE NATIONAL MONUMENT

The calcite crystals that glimmer within Jewel Cave are indeed a sight to behold. They are among the finest displays of natural crystals in the world. This brilliant work of nature lies far beneath the Black Hills throughout 193 miles of passageways, ranking Jewel Cave as the 2nd longest cave in the United States, and the 3rd longest cave in the world.

Established in 1890 and still a favored attraction, Hot Springs' historical Evans Plunge, the world's largest natural indoor warm water pool is where folks go to enjoy the warm, soothing mineral waters thought by many to be a remedy for aches and pains and, at the very least, a sort of refreshment for the soul.

The Mammoth Site in Hot Springs is the world's largest mammoth research facility where you can tour an active Paleontological dig site and view Ice Age fossils exhibited as they are found. The site has the largest concentration of mammoth remains in the world.

DEADWOOD

Historic Main Street, and all of Deadwood, is a National Historical Landmark. Nestled in a pine-fringed mountain gulch, this 1800s town is brimming with old-time saloons, museums, gold mines and even nightly gunfights. The way it was is very much the way it is in this fun-spirited town. With gaming halls offering poker, blackjack and slots, along with hotels and restaurants, the town has become one of the Black Hills' most popular entertainment destinations.

The legendary Wild Bill Hickok spent his share of time in South Dakota cleaning up some of the more notorious towns. Though much feared for his gun-toting abilities, Hickok was actually respected and well-liked by those who knew him. By all accounts, he had never shot anyone except in self-defense.

Calamity Jane, Poker Alice and Potato Creek Johnny were among the fortune seekers, dance hall girls, gamblers and gunslingers to join in Deadwood's first gold rush in 1875. The town's museums tell many a tale of these colorful legends, along with the history of Deadwood's booming days of mining.

SPEARFISH CANYON

The limestone rimmed canyon encompasses the simply awesome beauty of waterfalls, quaking aspens, fresh-smelling spruce, ponderosa pines and an array of wildflowers. Spearfish Creek meanders along the base of the scenic byway.

At the mouth of the canyon is the town of Spearfish, home of the High Plains Heritage Museum, Matthews Opera House and Black Hills State University.

Ask anyone who has traveled the way of Spearfish Canyon and they will attest that the pure misty water rushing over Roughlock Falls is a sight never forgotten.

Where the prairie finds its end and the skyward branches
reach their peak, a geological wonder rises from the landscape
northeast of Sturgis. Bear Butte is the much cherished place
known in Lakota as Mato Paha, or Bear Mountain. For the
Lakota and Cheyenne, Bear Butte is considered the birthplace
of their religions. It is customary for many tribes to journey
to these sacred slopes to pray, present offerings or vow a
personal sacrifice.

On the northern edge of the Hills, the historic Fort Meade was established at Sturgis. The city was once known as "Scoop Town" because soldiers from the fort were often "scooped," or wiped out by card sharks such as Poker Alice Tubbs.

Sprawled beside Rapid Creek in South Dakota's southwestern corner, Rapid City enjoys the benefits of being central to many of the state's attractions. The city's perimeter includes Mount Rushmore National Memorial, Badlands National Park, Black Hills National Forest and Custer State Park. Each of these areas can be a day trip by itself. Rapid City is also home to Storybook Island, Museum of Geology, The Journey Museum and Learning Center and 13 plus miles of biking/jogging paths following the creek through the city.

To the Lakota Indians and neighboring tribes who came to this barren region along the White River, the land was called "mako sica" or "land bad." The first white men of the area, French Canadian trappers, expressed their plight as "les mauvaises terres a traverser," or "bad land to travel across." Later settlers came up with "badlands." Today it is quite reverently, "The Badlands."

36

BADLANDS NATIONAL PARK

Like most national parks, Badlands is meant to be explored. Hiking, horseback riding and picnicking are enjoyable throughout the park. Favorite spots are Sheep Mountain Table, with its steep canyons and grassy tables, or Palmer Creek region with its sheer peaks and spires.

Five-hundred thousand years of erosion has created this rare and austerely beautiful place called the Badlands. The effects of time are perhaps no more evident than they are here. Unlike many volcanic eruptions and earthquakes, the Badlands evolved through a slow, yet no less amazing force known as erosion. Wind, Water and Time have joined forces to create this masterpiece of nature.

PIERRE

The hub of South Dakota's state government is in Pierre, its state capital. The stately capitol lies on the banks of the Missouri River; the city boasts that it's the only city on the Missouri that owns all of its waterfront. The capitol was dedicated in 1910, more than a decade after South Dakota became a state. Both North and South Dakota became states on the same date in 1889.

Photo Courtesy South Dakota State Historical Society

Oahe Dam, located just outside of Pierre, is the most impressive of all Missouri River basin projects. Constructed in 1948 to produce hydroelectric power, Oahe Dam is the world's second largest earth-rolled dam. The dam holds back the north-south flowing Missouri River waters half-way across the state and extends to the Cheyenne, Moreau and Grand River Valleys.

Lake Oahe is the largest of the four lakes created by hydroelectric dams on the Missouri River in South Dakota. The lake is a favorite for fishing, boating, swimming and water skiing.

MITCHELL CORN PALACE

Nowhere else in America, or the world for that matter, will one find the likes of the Mitchell Corn Palace. In a bold move to show farmers the opportunities that awaited in South Dakota, the first Corn Palace was built in 1892. The current structure was built in 1921.

The entire exterior of the Mitchell Corn Palace is redecorated every year, requiring nearly 3,000 bushels of corn, grains, and grasses which are hand-set. In most cases, the corn works are dated, with the year inscribed on the palace exterior.

As the pheasant population in South Dakota numbers around six million birds, one of the highest in the world; the supply accommodates the droves of avid sportsman.

The Ring-Necked pheasant's introduction to the state nearly a century ago was a successful one, with the bird thriving so well it was later named the official state bird.

Photo by Rita Trygstad

Best known as the childhood home of Laura Ingalls Wilder, De Smet is the setting for six of the great American author's books. The home of Charles and Caroline Ingalls and daughters Laura, Mary, Carrie and Grace has been carefully preserved and is furnished with some of the family's personal possessions. The Surveyors house, top left, is where the Ingalls family spent their first winter in 1879 after moving to South Dakota. The Laura Ingalls Wilder Homestead site, top right, is also located in De Smet.

VERMILLION/ SPIRIT MOUND

Vermillion is home to the University of South Dakota. The University was established in 1862 by the Dakota Territorial Legislature, minus the funds to operate it. In 1882 the community began supporting the school and one year later the legislature came through with the necessary funding.

The University is home to the National Music Museum which was founded in 1973 and is one of the great institutions of its kind. Its collection includes more than 14,800 American, European and non-Western instruments from virtually all cultures and historical periods.

The Omaha, Sioux and Otoe tribes believed that Spirit Mound was occupied by spirits that killed any human who came near.

Due to the extensive damming of the Missouri River, Spirit Mound is one of the few places which historians can identify as a precise spot upon which Lewis and Clark stood.

Yankton was the first capital of the Dakota Territory. It is named for the Yankton tribe of the Nakota (Sioux). Yankton is located on the Missouri River, just downstream from Gavins Point Dam. The Dam forms Lewis and Clark Lake, one of South Dakota's "Great Lakes" that have been formed by dams on the Missouri River.

A short drive across the Gavins Point Dam will take you to the Lewis and Clark Visitors Center. Even though it is actually in Nebraska, it would be worth the time to visit.

49

MISSOURI NATIONAL RECREATIONAL RIVER

The Missouri National Recreational River is located between South Dakota and Nebraska. It is comprised of 2 stretches of the river that are the only sections of the river between Montana and the mouth of the Missouri that remain undammed or unchannelized. In 1978 a 59 mile section of the Missouri River from Gavins Point Dam downriver to Ponca State Park (on the Nebraska side) was designated. In 1991 a 39 mile section between Fort Randall Dam downriver to the mouth of the Niobrara River was added. It is managed by the National Park Service.

On October 27, 1870 the stern wheel vessel, North Alabama, sunk at the mouth of the Vermillion River. It is one of many vessels that sunk carrying supplies up the Missouri from St. Louis in the latter half of the 1800s. The ships keel is still visible at times of low water level, a reminder of how difficult it was to settle the wild Dakota Territory.

The Fort Randall Military Post was established in 1856 in an effort to keep the peace on the expanding frontier. It was built on the south side of the Missouri River just below where the Fort Randall Dam stands today. Its remaining structure is a chapel, a mere shell of brick and mortar.

WATERTOWN/ ABERDEEN

Watertown is the fifth largest city in
South Dakota. It lies nearly due west
of Minneapolis in the northeast corner
of the state. It is home to the Redlin
Art Center which houses many of the
original works of art produced by
wildlife artist Terry Redlin.

Aberdeen is the third most populous
city in South Dakota. It is home to the
Milwaukee Road Depot built in 1911,
and the Dacotah Prairie Museum.

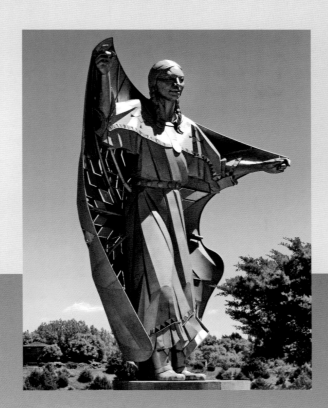

Chamberlain lies on the banks of Lake Francis Case, a dammed section of the Missouri River. It is home to Saint Joseph's Indian School which includes the Akta Lakota Museum and Cultural Center. The 50-foot statue of a Native American woman, Dignity, is located nearby.

It is said that the West begins after crossing the Missouri River at Chamberlain. Here a string of bridges span the Mighty Missouri, and the westward beauty of South Dakota begins to unfold.

SIOUX FALLS

There's so much to like about South Dakota's largest city. Perhaps it is because Sioux Falls has found a way to celebrate the present without forgetting its rich colorful past.

Sioux Falls' population accounts for nearly 30% of South Dakota's entire population. It is home to many financial services, banks and credit card servicing companies.

Sioux Falls is a regional shopping hub as well as home to attractions such as the Great Plains Zoo and the Sioux Falls Symphony.

The Big Sioux River runs through Sioux Falls, taking a meandering course around and through the city. Its namesake "Falls" are just north and slightly west of Downtown.

In the early 17th century, the Arikara, better known as the Ree Indians, first inhabited the land that is now South Dakota. The Lakota, having been driven from Minnesota and Wisconsin by the Ojibwa, began their movement to South Dakota in 1750. It is from the Lakota word, "dacotah," meaning "alliance of friends," that the state gets its name.

South Dakota's Native American tribes are a people of proud heritage, traditional rites and colorful pageantry. Today the tribes strive to maintain their cultural heritage through annual powwows. The powwow is the time-honored tradition of Native Americans. The ceremony is always one of great color and grandeur. It is a time for reflection on their rich heritage, to dance in celebration, and to enjoy the company of family and friends.

SOUTH DAKOTA WILDLIFE

Its long, sweeping tail, brilliant feathers and characteristic ring-around-the-neck sets South Dakota's state bird apart from the rest. The immigrant pheasant, originally from China, was first introduced into the state in 1908.

Sharp-tailed grouse, often called Sharptails, and the greater prairie chickens are collectively referred to as prairie grouse. They are primarily interspersed across the short grass prairie of central and western South Dakota.

Northern bobwhite quail are also found in the extreme southeastern part of the state.

SOUTH DAKOTA WILDLIFE

The bull elk takes refuge primarily in the Black Hills of South Dakota with herds consisting of over 6,000 Rocky Mountain elk. These majestic beauties, with their massive crown of antlers, are one of the largest members of the deer family. A mature male stands about five feet at its shoulder and weighs as much as 1,000 pounds.

The graceful, quick-footed white-tail deer rouses the interest of hunters and nature lovers alike. Come fall, sportsmen from neighboring states converge on Western South Dakota for the time-honored quest of bringing home a trophy buck. Large numbers of deer inhabit the state, where most are readily spotted in grassy meadows and beside streams.

Bighorn Sheep were originally indigenous to the Black Hills of South Dakota before the arrival of the white man. They were reintroduced in 1922 when eight Rocky Mountain Bighorns were released in Custer State Park. This herd grew until its demise for unknown reasons in the late 1950s. Additional efforts began in the 1960s to relocate and reintroduce Bighorns in the Black Hills. Due to their limited numbers there is little hunting of Bighorns allowed in South Dakota.

North America's fastest land animal, the prong-horn, is capable of running up to 55 miles per hour. Prominent in South Dakota's parks, the pronghorn wields an imposing, almost regal, stature. They are shy and this is enough to keep the pronghorn safe from predators.

Perched on mountain tops and rocky hillsides are the mountain goats so prevalent in South Dakota's Black Hills and Mount Rushmore areas. The white-shagged coat with slender, backward-curving horns were brought to Custer State Park in the early 1920s and later migrated to other regions of the state.

The bison, among the largest creatures to graze South Dakota prairies, were nearly extinct a century ago. Today large herds roam freely, especially along the eastern edge of the Black Hills in Custer State Park and Wind Cave National Park. With the prairies vital to its existence, it has been estimated that one bison requires nearly 100 acres of grasses to survive.

Prairie Dogs are burrowing rodents that live in large colonies in the grasslands of central and western North America. They have a complex system of communication that includes a variety of pitched warning barks that signal different types of predators.

The prairie rattlesnake is the only venomous snake native to South Dakota. They live in all areas of western South Dakota. They can be found in grassy fields and wooded mountains.

In the quiet of an open prairie, the most majestic of
beasts grazes beneath a western sky. To the cowboy,
a good horse was his partner, his means of travel and his
best friend. Faithful, honest and hard-working – the horse
is among the most virtuous of creatures. Its very spirit
embodies all that is great about the American West.
This is South Dakota!